Janice VanCleave's
WILD, WACKY, and WEIRD
Science Experiments

Janice VanCleave's Wild, Wacky, and Weird CHEMISTRY EXPERIMENTS

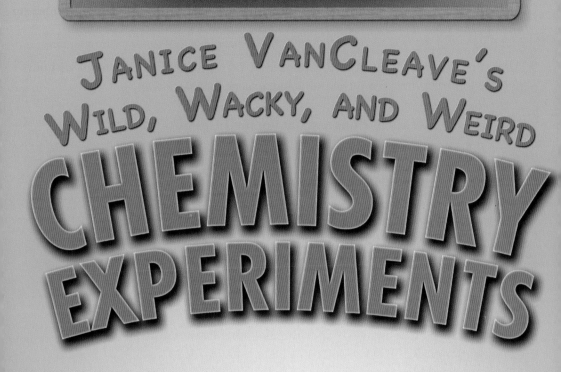

ROSEN PUBLISHING

New York

This edition published in 2017 by:
The Rosen Publishing Group, Inc.
29 East 21st Street
New York, NY 10010

Library of Congress Cataloging-in-Publication Data

Names: VanCleave, Janice Pratt.
Title: Janice VanCleave's wild, wacky, and weird chemistry experiments / Janice VanCleave.
Other titles: Wild, wacky, and weird chemistry experiments
Description: New York : Rosen Central, 2017. | Series: Janice VanCleave's wild, wacky, and weird science experiments | Audience: Grades 7-12. | Includes bibliographical references and index.
Identifiers: LCCN 2016008912| ISBN 9781477789711 (library bound) | ISBN 9781477789698 (pbk.) | ISBN 9781477789704 (6-pack)
Subjects: LCSH: Chemistry--Experiments--Juvenile literature.
Classification: LCC QD43 .V36 2017 | DDC 540.78--dc23
LC record available at http://lccn.loc.gov/2016008912

Manufactured in China

Experiments first published in *Janice VanCleave's 202 Oozing, Bubbling, Dripping, and Bouncing Experiments* by John Wiley & Sons, Inc. copyright © 1996 Janice VanCleave.

CONTENTS

INTRODUCTION

Chemistry is the study of the way materials are put together and their behavior under different conditions. Matter makes up everything in the universe. Chemists study all this matter to learn what it is made of and how it reacts.

The people who choose chemistry as a career do a variety of work. Food chemists study the ingredients in what we eat, doctors study biochemistry and the reactions that take place in the body, and forensic chemists work with crime scene evidence. All these people have something in common: They are constantly asking questions to learn even more about chemistry.

This book is a collection of science experiments about chemistry. Why do bubbles escape from a bottle of soda? How can you test for carbon dioxide in exhaled breath? Why does water bead on certain surfaces? You will find the answers to these and many other questions by doing the experiments in this book.

How to Use This Book

Before you get started, be sure to read each experiment completely before starting. The following sections are included for all the experiments.

» **PURPOSE:** *The basic goals for the experiment.*

» **MATERIALS:** *A list of supplies you will need.*

You will experience less frustration and more fun if you gather all the necessary materials for the experiments before you begin. You lose your train of thought when you have to shop and search for supplies.

» **PROCEDURE:** *Step-by-step instructions on how to perform the experiment.*

Follow each step very carefully, never skip steps, and do not add your own. **Safety is of the utmost importance, and by reading the experiment before starting, then following the instructions exactly, you can feel confident that no unexpected results will occur. Ask an adult to help you when you are working with anything sharp or hot. If adult supervisor is required, it will be noted in the experiment.**

» **RESULTS:** *An explanation stating exactly what is expected to happen.*

This is an immediate learning tool. If the expected results are achieved, you will know that you did the experiment correctly. If your results are not the same as described in the experiment, carefully read the instructions and start over from the first step.

INTRODUCTION

» **WHY?** *An explanation of why the results were achieved.*
You will be rewarded with successful experiments if you read each experiment carefully, follow the steps in order, and do not substitute materials.

THE SCIENTIFIC METHOD

Scientists identify a problem or observe an event. Then they seek solutions or explanations through research and experimentation. By doing the experiments in this book, you will learn to follow experimental steps and make observations. You will also learn many scientific principles that have to do with chemistry.

In the process, the things you see or learn may lead you to new questions. For example, perhaps you have completed the experiment that looks at splatter to determine why moon craters are spread out. Now you wonder what would happen if you dropped each pebble from different heights. That's great! Every scientist is curious and asks new questions about what they learn. When you design a new experiment, it is a good idea to follow the scientific method.

1. Ask a question.

2. Do some research about your question. What do you already know?

3. Come up with a hypothesis, or a possible answer to your question.

4. Design an experiment to test your hypothesis. Make sure the experiment is repeatable.

5. Collect the data and make observations.

6. Analyze your results.

7. Reach a conclusion. Did your results support your hypothesis?

Many times the experiment leads to more questions and a new experiment.

Always remember that when devising your own science experiment, have a knowledgeable adult review it with you before trying it out. Ask them to supervise it as well.

BUILDING BLOCKS

PURPOSE To build a model of a lithium atom.

MATERIALS scissors
ruler
stiff wire
red, green, and yellow modeling clay
string

PROCEDURE

1. Cut two pieces of wire, one 12 inches (30 cm) long and the other 18 inches (45 cm) long.

2. Bend and shape the wires into two circles as shown. Use clay to support the circles.

3. Cut a 6-inch (15-cm) piece of string and tie the string to the top of the inner wire circle.

4. Mold small balls from the clay. Make three red balls, three yellow, and four green.

5. Press two of the red balls onto the inner circle of wire, one on each side.

6. Press the third ball of red clay onto the outer circle of wire, on the right side.

7. Press the yellow clay balls and the green clay balls together around the string so that they are hanging at the center of the circle. Trim away any excess string.

8

RESULTS You have made a three-dimensional model of a lithium atom, showing the position of the atom's electrons (red), protons (yellow), and neutrons (green).

WHY? Atoms are the smallest building blocks of matter (any substance that takes up space and has weight). Atoms are made of smaller particles called protons (which have a positive charge), electrons (which have a negative charge), and neutrons (which are neutral, having neither a positive nor a negative charge). A lithium atom has three protons and four neutrons in its nucleus (the central part of the atom) and three electrons outside the nucleus.

BONDED

PURPOSE To make a model of the physical structure of methane.

MATERIALS 4 toothpicks
1 large black gumdrop
4 small white gumdrops

PROCEDURE

1. Stick the toothpicks into the black gumdrop. Space the toothpicks so that they are an equal distance from each other.

2. Place a white gumdrop on the end of each toothpick

RESULTS You have made a three-dimensional model of a methane molecule.

WHY? Methane is a hydrocarbon molecule. Hydrocarbon molecules are composed of carbon and hydrogen atoms. Each carbon atom in a hydrocarbon molecule has four bonds (connections between atoms) that are equally spaced, and each hydrogen atom has one bond. Methane is the simplest hydrocarbon molecule. In your methane model, the single black gumdrop represents one carbon atom bonded (attached) to four hydrogen atoms represented by the white gumdrops. The chemical formula used to represent methane is $CH_4 \bullet$ The formula, like the model you made, shows that the methane molecule has one carbon atom and four hydrogen atoms.

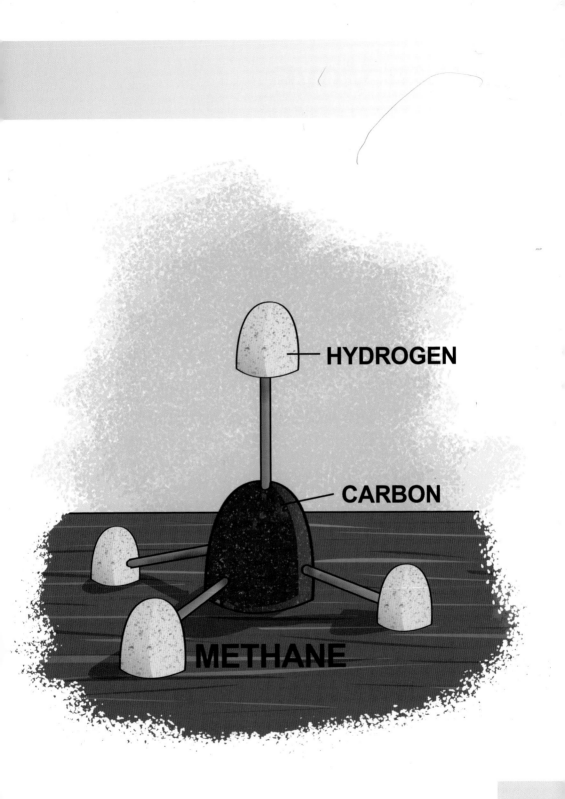

ON THE MOVE

PURPOSE To determine if water molecules are in constant motion.

MATERIALS measuring cup
tap water
¼ teaspoon (1 ml) salt
green food coloring
spoon
clear juice glass
index card

PROCEDURE

1. Measure ¼ cup (60 ml) water into the measuring cup. Add salt and 5 drops of coloring. Stir.

2. Fill the glass one-fourth full with water.

3. Tilt the glass, and slowly pour the green salt water down the side.

4. Cover the top of the glass with the index card, and place the glass where it will not be disturbed.

5. Observe the glass as often as possible for 2 days.

RESULTS At first, the green salty water settles to the bottom of the glass and the clear water floats on top. After 2 days, all of the liquid in the glass is green.

WHY? The green salty water sinks under the clear water because the salt water is heavier than the clear water. With time, the liquids mix together. This mixing is caused by the constant motion of the water molecules. The mixing of molecules because of molecular motion is called diffusion.

WATER

GREEN SALTY WATER

PURPOSE To determine if water molecules in liquid water fit tightly together.

MATERIALS clear drinking glass
plate
tap water
paper towel
1-teaspoon (5-ml) measuring spoon
table salt

PROCEDURE

1. Place the glass on the plate.

2. Fill the glass to the brim with water. Stop adding the water when a tiny stream of water starts to flow over the side of the glass. (If you look sideways at the surface of the water, you can see it "bulging" over the top of the glass.)

3. Without moving the glass or plate, carefully blot up the water in the plate with the paper towel.

4. Fill the measuring spoon with salt.

5. Very slowly sprinkle salt crystals into the glass of water. If you use the entire spoonful, fill the spoon again.

6. Continue to add salt until water spills over the top of the glass.

14

RESULTS The amount of salt that can be added before the water spills depends on the size of the glass.

WHY? The grains of salt are made of tiny molecules. These molecules break away from each other and freely move around in the water. The water molecules in liquid water are connected in such a way that small empty pockets are formed. Separate salt molecules are small enough to easily fit into the spaces between the connected water molecules.

BEADS

PURPOSE To determine why water forms beads on certain surfaces.

MATERIALS saucer
baby powder
red, blue, or green food coloring in a dropper bottle

PROCEDURE

1. Cover the saucer with a thin layer of powder.

2. Place several drops of food coloring on the powder layer.

NOTE: Keep the results of this activity for the next experiment, "Spreader."

RESULTS The food coloring forms colored balls on the powder's surface.

WHY? Food coloring is colored water. Water forms beads on certain surfaces because of the surface tension of liquids. Surface tension is the tendency of molecules to cling together at the surface of a liquid to form a skinlike film. The surface molecules tend to pull inward on each other to form a sphere. This occurs when water molecules are more attracted to each other than to the surface they touch.

SPREADER

PURPOSE To demonstrate the decrease of water's surface tension.

MATERIALS dishwashing liquid
saucer
toothpick
saucer with beads of colored water from the previous experiment, "Beads"

PROCEDURE

1. Pour a drop of dishwashing liquid on the saucer.

2. Dip the end of the toothpick into the drop of dishwashing liquid.

3. Touch the wet end of the toothpick to several of the colored beads on the powder.

RESULTS The beads break open and spread out.

WHY? The detergent molecules in the dishwashing liquid move between the water molecules that make up the surface of the colored beads. The presence of the detergent molecules decreases the strong attractive forces between the water molecules. Thus, the surface tension of the water decreases, and the beads break apart.

DISHWA
LIQU

DIPPER

PURPOSE To determine when and why the surface of water dips in the center.

MATERIALS paper hole-punch
sheet of printer paper
small glass with no more than a 2-inch (5-cm) diameter (a candle holder or an egg holder will work)
tap water

PROCEDURE

1. Use the hole-punch to cut 3 or 4 circles from the paper.

2. Fill the glass about three-quarters full with water.

3. When the water is calm, place the paper circles on the surface in the center.

RESULTS After a few seconds the paper moves to the side.

WHY? In the partially filled glass, surface water molecules are more attracted to the sides of the glass than to each other. This attraction causes the surface water molecules to be pulled toward the glass, carrying the lightweight paper circles with them. The water rises up the sides of the glass, causing the surface of the water to dip in the center.

BULGE

PURPOSE To determine when and why the surface of water bulges in the center.

MATERIALS paper hole-punch
sheet of printer paper
small glass with no more than a 2-inch (5- cm) diameter (a candle holder or an egg holder will work)
saucer
tap water
toothpick

PROCEDURE

1. Use the hole-punch to cut 3 or 4 circles from the paper.

2. Place the glass in the saucer.

3. Fill the glass to overflowing with water. The surface of the water should bulge above the sides of the glass.

4. When the water is calm, place the paper circles on the surface of the water in the center.

5. Use the toothpick to move the circles toward the edge carefully, then release them. Be sure that you do not force the water over the edge of the glass.

6. Repeat the previous step.

RESULTS The paper circles continue to move toward the center of the water.

WHY? In the overfilled glass, the surface water molecules above the glass pull on each other. The direction of this pull creates a bulge on the water's surface and pulls the paper circles toward the peak of the bulge.

TUG-OF-WAR

PURPOSE To determine why some materials get wetter than others.

MATERIALS drinking glass   eyedropper
liquid cooking oil   tap water

PROCEDURE

1. Turn the glass upside down on a table and rub a drop of oil on one half of its bottom surface.

2. Fill the eyedropper with water and squeeze a drop of water on both the oiled and the unoiled areas of the glass.

3. Observe the shape of the water drops.

RESULTS The water drop spreads out and flattens on the clean surface of the glass. The drop of water on the oiled surface is more ball-like in shape.

WHY? The shape of the water drops is due to two different forces, cohesion and adhesion. Cohesion is the force of attraction between like molecules, such as water molecules. The water molecules pull on each other, which gives the drops of liquid a spherical (ball-like) shape. Adhesion is the force of attraction between different kinds of molecules, such as glass and water molecules. Glass strongly attracts the water molecules, which causes the water drop to flatten and spread out. Water is said to "wet" a surface if it spreads out on the material. The wetting ability of water depends on the adhesive force between the surface molecules and the water molecules. The adhesion between an oily surface and water molecules is very small, and thus a drop of water on an oily surface retains its spherical shape.

UPHILL CLIMBERS

PURPOSE To determine if water can rise in a vertical paper towel.

MATERIALS scissors
2-by-8-inch (5-by-20-cm) strip of paper
towel
red food coloring
transparent tape
pencil
tap water
ruler
glass jar, about 6 inches (15 cm) tall

PROCEDURE

1. Place a drop of red food coloring 2 inches (5 cm) from one end of the paper strip.

2. Tape the uncolored end of the paper to the center of the pencil. Roll some of the paper around the pencil.

3. Pour about 1 inch (2.5 cm) of water into the jar.

4. Lower the paper into the jar. Unroll the strip until the bottom edge just touches the water.

RESULTS The water dissolves the red coloring as it rises in the paper strip. The red coloring spreads outward and upward.

WHY? The paper is made of tiny fibers. The spacing of the fibers forms tubelike structures throughout the paper. The water can be seen zigzagging through these spaces. The adhesive attraction of water to the paper is strong enough to move the water up the sides of the fiber tubes against the downward pull of gravity. The water molecules clinging to the fiber then pull the lower water molecules up the center of the tube. The movement of the water up through the tiny tubes is called capillary action.

BLOW UP

PURPOSE To determine if a gas fills an open container.

MATERIALS drinking straw
empty glass soda bottle
9-inch (22.5-cm) round balloon

PROCEDURE

1. Hold the top of the balloon and push the bottom of the balloon inside the bottle.

2. Insert the straw into the bottle beside the balloon.

3. Blow into the mouth of the balloon.

RESULTS The balloon inflates and air is felt coming out of the straw.

WHY? The air surrounding the bottle, like all gases, is in constant motion. This moving gas enters, spreads out, and fills the open bottle and straw. As you inflate the balloon inside the bottle, it pushes against the air inside the bottle. The pressure from the balloon forces the air in the bottle out the straw.

Blow Up

CLINGERS

PURPOSE To determine if water can flow at an angle.

MATERIALS 18-inch (45-cm) piece of cotton kite string
measuring cup with spout and handle
tap water
drinking glass
cookie sheet
helper

PROCEDURE

1. Tie one end of the string around the top of the measuring cup's handle.

2. Fill the cup with water.

3. Wet the entire length of the string with water.

4. Set the glass in the center of the cookie sheet.

5. Lay the string over the spout of the measuring cup.

6. Ask your helper to hold the free end of the string against the inside of the glass.

7. Separate the cup and glass so the string is tight.

8. Raise the bottom of the cup about 12 inches (30 cm) above the cookie sheet.

9. Slowly pour the water out of the cup.

RESULTS The water flows down the string into the glass.

WHY? The water in the wet string attracts the molecules in the falling water. The surface tension on the outside of the flowing water holds the water close to the string as it flows down the slanted string.

MAGIC PAPER

PURPOSE To observe the attraction between molecules.

MATERIALS sheet of printer paper
2-by-6-inch (5-by-15-cm) piece of newspaper
rubber cement
talcum powder
scissors (Do not use school scissors.)

PROCEDURE

1. Lay the printer paper on a table and place the newspaper in its center.

2. Evenly spread a thin, solid covering of rubber cement over the top surface of the newspaper.

3. Allow the rubber cement to dry for 5 minutes.

4. Sprinkle talcum powder evenly over the cement.

5. Cut the newspaper into two 1-by-6-inch (2.5-by-15-cm) strips.

6. Place the strips together with the powdered surfaces touching.

7. Cut across one end of the strips by inserting the paper as far into the scissors as possible and cutting with the largest part of the blade.

8. Gently raise the other end of one of the strips.

9. Hold up only the raised edge, allowing the strip to hang.

RESULTS One long strip is formed.

WHY? The powder is used to cover the cement so that the pieces do not stick together. When the sharp edges of the scissors cut the paper, the pressure applied by the blades pushes a small amount of rubber cement along the cut surface. The adhesion between the cement molecules is great. These molecules are able to bridge the gap between the cut pieces and hold them together.

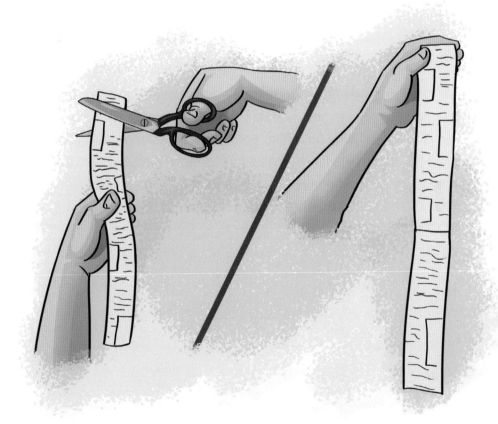

ESCAPING BUBBLES

PURPOSE To determine why bubbles escape from a glass of soda.

MATERIALS baby food jar
soda, any flavor

PROCEDURE

1. 1. Fill the jar one-half full with soda.

2. 2. Set the jar on a table and observe the liquid.

RESULTS Small bubbles of gas continuously rise to the top of the liquid.

WHY? Carbonated beverages are made by dissolving large amounts of carbon dioxide gas in flavored water. This excess amount of carbon dioxide gas is able to stay in the liquid because it is pushed with high pressure into the bottle and the bottle is immediately sealed. In the open glass the pressure on the soda is much less than in the closed bottle. Thus, carbon dioxide bubbles form in the soda, rise to the surface, and escape into the air.

Escaping Bubbles

LIMEWATER

PURPOSE To make a testing solution for carbon dioxide.

MATERIALS 2 quart (liter) glass jars with lids
distilled water
1 tablespoon (15 ml) lime (also called calcium oxide; used to make pickles)
spoon
masking tape
marking pen
adult helper

PROCEDURE

1. 1. Fill one jar with distilled water.

2. 2. Ask an adult to add the lime to the water and stir.

CAUTION: Do not get powdered lime in your nose or eyes. It can damage these soft tissues.

3. Place the lid securely on the jar. Allow the solution to stand overnight.

4. On the following day, pour the clear liquid into the second jar. Be careful not to pour out any of the lime that has settled on the bottom of the jar.

5. Use the tape and marking pen to label the second jar Limewater. Place the lid securely on the second jar and save it for other experiments.

RESULTS The liquid is milky white at first. After standing overnight, the liquid is clear.

WHY? The lime is a solute (dissolving material) and the water a solvent (dissolving medium). The mixing of a solute and solvent produces a solution. In the lime solution, the undissolved particles of lime are temporarily suspended in the water, making it appear milky. It takes time for all of the tiny particles to settle. The clear liquid is a saturated solution, meaning that no more solute (lime) can dissolve in the solvent (water). It must be covered to prevent the carbon dioxide in the air from dissolving in it.

Lime

Lime Water

CHEMICAL BREATH

PURPOSE To test for the presence of carbon dioxide gas in exhaled breath.

MATERIALS clear drinking glass
limewater (from Experiment 98)
drinking straw

PROCEDURE

1. Fill the glass one-fourth full with limewater.

2. Use the straw to blow into the limewater.

CAUTION: Do not drink the limewater.

3. Continue to blow into the liquid until a distinctive color is observed.

RESULTS The limewater turns from clear to a milky color.

WHY? Limewater always turns milky when mixed with carbon dioxide. The chemical in the limewater combines with the carbon dioxide gas in the breath to form limestone, a white powder that does not dissolve in water. If the solution is allowed to stand for several hours, the powdery limestone will fall to the bottom of the glass.

Chemical Breath

Super Chain

PURPOSE To observe a physical change.

MATERIALS lined notebook paper   pencil
                 scissors   ruler

PROCEDURE

1. On the paper, draw and cut out a rectangle that is 4 inches (10 cm) wide and 12 lines long.

2. Fold the rectangle in half lengthwise, perpendicular to the lines.

3. Cut across the fold at points A and B as shown. Stop about ¼ inch (½ cm) from the edge of the paper.

4. Cut along each of the printed lines alternating from the folded edge to the open edge. Be sure to stop ¼ inch (½ cm) from the edge.

5. Start at point B and cut the folded edge off of the paper ending at point A. Do not cut the folded edge from the two ends.

6. Carefully stretch the paper open.

RESULTS The shape of the paper changed from a rectangle to an open chain-like structure.

WHY? Cutting the paper results in a physical change (a change that does not produce a new substance). The zigzag structure allows the paper to stretch out into a large super chain.

BREAKDOWN

PURPOSE To change the natural form of an egg white.

MATERIALS raw egg
2-quart (2-liter) bowl
fork
adult helper

CAUTION: Always wash your hands after touching an uncooked egg. It may contain harmful bacteria.

PROCEDURE

1. Ask an adult to help you separate the yolk from the egg white, placing the egg white in the bowl.

2. Allow the egg white to sit undisturbed at room temperature for 20 minutes.

3. Dip the fork into the egg white, and lift the fork above the bowl. Observe the texture and color of the egg white on the fork.

4. Return the egg white to the bowl, and with a quick whipping motion, use the fork to beat the egg white.

5. After 50 strokes, observe the egg white again.

RESULTS Before beating, the egg white actually has a pale yellow color and a slimy texture. After beating, the color is white, and the texture is soft and foamy. The foamy egg white takes up more space than the slimy egg white.

WHY? Denaturing means to change something from its natural form. In its natural form, the egg white contains about 85 percent water and about 10 percent protein. It is the protein (large molecules composed of chains of smaller molecules) that is denatured by the whipping action. The protein molecules are similar to balls of yam, and beating the egg white causes the balls of proteins to unravel. The shape of this new unwound protein molecule traps air and thus forms a foam that can be three times the original size of the molecule. The color is also changed as the molecules are re-arranged.

COLORED EGGS

PURPOSE To determine the role of vinegar in dyeing eggshells.

MATERIALS 1-pint (500-ml) jar
tap water
measuring spoons
blue food coloring
2 drinking glasses
marking pen

masking tape
white vinegar (5%)
large spoon
2 hard-boiled eggs
paper towel

PROCEDURE

1. Fill the jar half full with water.

2. Add 2 teaspoons (10 ml) of food coloring to the water and stir. Pour half of the colored water into one glass and half into the other.

3. Use the tape and marking pen to label one of the glasses With Vinegar. Add 1 teaspoon (5 ml) of vinegar to this glass and stir.

4. Label the other glass Without Vinegar.

5. Use the large spoon to place one egg in each of the glasses.

6. Allow the eggs to remain undisturbed for 2 minutes.

7. Remove the eggs, place them on the paper towel, and allow them to air dry. Observe their color.

RESULTS The egg soaked in the dye solution containing vinegar is a darker blue than the egg soaked in the dye solution without vinegar.

WHY? To dye an object, the molecules of dye must stick to the surface of the object. Vinegar (acetic acid and water) reacts with the layer of protein molecules covering the surface of the eggshell so that the surface becomes positively charged and attracts the negatively charged dye molecules, causing the darker blue color. The egg in the solution without vinegar has some color because some of the dye molecules become lodged in crevices in the eggshell.

Wash Out!

PURPOSE To determine how stains are cleaned by enzymes found in detergents.

MATERIALS 1 quart (liter) glass jar
tap water
measuring spoon
powdered laundry detergent with enzymes
large spoon
marking pen
masking tape
1 fresh, peeled hard-boiled egg
magnifying lens

PROCEDURE

1. Fill the jar three-fourths full with tap water.

2. Add 1 tablespoon (15 ml) of the laundry detergent to the jar of water and stir.

3. Place the egg in the jar and put it in a warm area, such as near a window with direct sunlight.

4. Each day, for 7 or more days, lift the egg out of the jar with the spoon and use the magnifying lens for close-up inspection.

5. Each day, replace the eggs in a fresh solution of the mixture of laundry detergent and water.

RESULTS The egg has large craters on its surface.

WHY? Tangled strings of some proteins get wrapped around the fibers in clothes, causing stains. For these stains to be removed, the proteins must be broken into smaller pieces. Enzymes, like those in the detergent used in this experiment, are biological catalysts (chemicals that change the rate of a chemical reaction without being changed themselves). They cut the long strands of proteins (as they did on the surface of the egg) without affecting the cloth fibers. These cut pieces slip out of the cloth and are washed away with the dirt.

RUBBERY

PURPOSE To demonstrate the effect of vinegar on bones.

MATERIALS cooked chicken leg
quart (liter) jar with lid
white vinegar (5%)
adult helper

PROCEDURE

1. Ask an adult to cut as much of the meat away from the chicken leg bone as possible.

2. Examine the flexibility of the bone by trying to bend it with your fingers.

3. Place the cleaned bone in the jar.

4. Cover the bone with vinegar.

5. Secure the lid on the jar.

6. After 24 hours, remove the bone from the jar and examine it for flexibility.

7. Replace the bone in the vinegar.

8. Examine the bone for flexibility each day for 7 days.

RESULTS The flexibility of the bone increases daily. At the end of the test period, the bone feels very rubbery.

WHY? Vinegar, which is an acid, reacts chemically with the bone. It removes the calcium compounds in the bone. The bone becomes rubbery as the result of the loss of calcium. This indicates that calcium is the chemical element in bones that gives them strength and firmness.

SWEETER

PURPOSE To compare the sweetness of sugar and artificial sweeteners.

MATERIALS blindfold (a long scarf will work)
packet of Nutrasweet®
packet of Sweet'n Low®
packet of table sugar
plate
3 clean cotton swabs
cup of tap water
helper

PROCEDURE

NOTE: Never taste anything in a laboratory setting unless you are sure that it does not contain harmful chemicals or materials.

1. Place the blindfold over your helper's eyes.

2. Open each packet of sweetener and pour the contents in separate piles on the plate. Lay each packet next to its sweetener to identify it.

3. Moisten a cotton swab with water, lay it on a sweetener in the plate, then hand it to your helper.

4. Instruct your helper to put the swab in his or her mouth, taste the sweetener, and note its sweetness.

5. Have your helper drink a small amount of water to rinse the sweetener out of his or her mouth.

6. Repeat steps 3 through 5 with each of the other two sweeteners. Ask your helper to compare the sweetness of each sample.

RESULTS The sweetest-tasting sweetener is Sweet'n Low. Table sugar is the least sweet.

WHY? Sweet'n Low is saccharin, a chemical that tastes about 300 times sweeter than sucrose (table sugar). The chemical aspartame, with the trade name Nutrasweet, is about 200 times sweeter than sucrose.

LUMPY

PURPOSE To demonstrate why milk curdles.

MATERIALS ¼ cup (63 ml) whole milk
small bowl
2 tablespoons (30 ml) white vinegar
spoon
timer

PROCEDURE

1. Pour the milk into the bowl.

2. Add the vinegar and stir.

3. Allow the contents of the bowl to stand for about 5 minutes.

RESULTS The milk separates into white solid lumps mixed with a thin, watery liquid. Most of the lumps sink to the bottom of the bowl.

WHY? Milk contains particles of casein (milk protein). The casein particles are negatively charged. Vinegar is an acid; like all acids, it contains positively charged hydrogen particles. Negative and positive charges are attracted to each other. Thus, the negatively charged casein particles and the positively charged hydrogen particles combine, forming white lumps. Allowing milk to become warm produces the same results that adding vinegar does. The sugar in the milk changes into an acid. The positive hydrogens in the acid attract the negative casein. In both cases, the milk separates into white lumps called curds (the solid part of milk) and a thin watery liquid called whey (the liquid part of milk).

Lumpy

FADED

PURPOSE To determine how sunlight affects color.

MATERIALS scissors
ruler
sheet of red construction paper
stiff paper, such as a file folder

PROCEDURE

1. Cut a 6-by-6-inch (15-by-15-cm) square from both the construction paper and the stiff paper.

2. Cut a large star from the center of the square of stiff paper.

3. Lay the square of stiff paper, with the star section removed, over the square of red paper.

4. Place the pieces of paper near a window that receives direct sunlight.

5. After 2 days, remove the stiff paper.

RESULTS A light red or pink star shape is in the center of the red paper.

WHY? The energy from the sunlight causes some color pigments to fade (get lighter in color). Different chemical reactions occur when sunlight is absorbed by a substance. The fading of colors is generally the result of the combination of oxygen in the air with the color pigment. This fading happens very slowly without the sunlight, but with the sunlight, it occurs quickly.

Faded

GLOSSARY

ACID Substance that turns cabbage indicator red.

ADHESION The force of attraction between different kinds of molecules.

ATOMS The smallest building blocks of matter.

BOND The electrical attraction between atoms that connects them.

CAPILLARY ACTION The movement of water or any liquid through a tiny tube.

COHESION The force of attraction between like molecules.

DENATURE To change something from its natural form.

DIFFUSION The mixing of molecules because of molecular motion.

ELECTRON The negatively charged particle in an atom.

HYDROCARBON A molecule that contains hydrogen and carbon atoms.

MATTER Any substance that takes up space and has weight.

MOLECULE The smallest particle of a substance; made of one or more atoms.

NEUTRON The neutral charged particle in an atom.

NUCLEUS The central part of an atom.

PHYSICAL CHANGE A change that does not produce a new substance.

PROTEIN Large molecules composed of chains of smaller molecules; essential to all living cells for the growth and repair of tissue.

PROTON The positive charge in an atom.

SATURATED SOLUTION A solution in which no more solute will dissolve.

SOLUTE Material that dissolves in a solvent.

SOLUTION The combination of a solute and a solvent.

SOLVENT The material in which a solute dissolves.

SURFACE TENSION The tendency of liquid molecules to cling together at the surface to form a skinlike film across the surface of the liquid.

FOR MORE INFORMATION

American Association for the Advancement of Science (AAAS)
  1200 New York Ave NW
  Washington, DC 20005
  (202) 326-6400
  website: http://www.aaas.org
  The AAAS has been promoting the advancement of science for over 150
  years. Take part in Family Science Days, learn about the latest discoveries through their daily Science Update, or see their choices for the best
  science books for kids.

American Chemical Society (ACS)
  1155 Sixteenth Street, NW
  Washington, DC 20036
  (800) 333-9511
  website: http://www.acs.org
  The American Chemical Society has free educational resources, includ-
  ing experiments and games in their Adventures in Chemistry program;
  high school chemistry clubs; the Chemistry Olympiad competition for
  students, and Project SEED summer research programs. They educate
  the public with National Chemistry Week.

Chemical Institute of Canada
  222 Queen Street, Suite 400
  Ottawa, ON K1P 5Vp
  Canada
  (888) 542-2242
  website: http://www.cheminst.ca
  The Chemical Institute of Canada provides information about available

science fairs, scholarships, and the Canadian Chemistry Contest.

National Science Foundation (NSF)
4201 Wilson Boulevard
Arlington, VA 22230
(703) 292-5111
website: http://www.nsf.gov
The NSF is dedicated to science, engineering, education. Learn how to be a Citizen Scientist, read about the latest scientific discoveries, and discover the newest innovations in technology.

The Society for Science and the Public
Student Science
1719 N Street, N.W.
Washington, D.C. 20036
(800) 552-4412
website: https://student.societyforscience.org
The Society for Science and the Public presents many science project resources, such as science news for students, the latest updates on the Intel Science Talent Search and the Intel International Science and Engineering Fair, and information about cool jobs and doing science.

WEBSITES

Because of the changing nature of Internet links, Rosen Publishing has developed an online list of websites related to the subject of this book. This site is updated regularly. Please use this link to access this list:

http://www.rosenlinks.com/JVCW/chem

FOR FURTHER READING

Ardley, Neil. *101 Great Science Experiments*. New York: DK Ltd., 2014.

Ball, Nate. *The Science Unfair* (Alien in My Pocket). New York: Harper, 2014.

Biskup, Agnieszka. *Super Cool Chemical Reaction Activities with Max Axiom* (Max Axiom Science and Engineering Activities). North Mankato, MN: Capstone Press, 2015.

Buczynski, Sandy. *Designing a Winning Science Fair Project* (Information Explorer Junior). Ann Arbor, MI: Cherry Lake Publishing, 2014.

Henneberg, Susan. *Creating Science Fair Projects with Cool New Digital Tools* (Way Beyond PowerPoint: Making 21st Century Presentations). New York: Rosen Central, 2014.

Margles, Samantha. *Mythbusters Science Fair Book*. New York: Scholastic, 2011.

Mercer, Bobby. *Junk Drawer Chemistry: 50 Awesome Experiments that Don't Cost a Thing*. Chicago: Chicago Review Press, 2015.

Navarro, Paula. *Incredible Experiments with Chemical Reactions and Mixtures* (Magic Science). Hauppague, NY: Barron's Educational Series, 2014.

Ruff Ruffman's *44 Favorite Science Activities* (Fetch! with Ruff Ruffman). Somerville MA: Candlewick Press, 2015.

Thomas, Isabel. *Experiments with Materials* (Read and Experiment). Chicago: Heinemann Raintree, 2016.

Wheeler-Toppen, Jodi. *Cool Chemistry Activities for Girls* (Girls Science Club). Mankato, MN: Capstone Press, 2012.

INDEX

Janice VanCleave's Wild, Wacky, and Weird Chemistry Experiments

M

methane
> description of, 10
> physical structure of, 10–11

milk, curdling of, 52–53
molecular motion, 13
molecule/molecules
> attraction between, 32–33
> hydrocarbon, 10

N

neutrons, 9
Nutrasweet, 51

P

physical change, observation of, 40
protons, 9

S

soda, escaping bubbles and, 34–35
solute, 37
solvent, 37
stains, cleaning of, 46–47
sucrose, 51
sugar vs. artificial sweeteners,
> 50–51

sunlight, effect of on color, 54–55
surface molecules, 16

surface tension, 16
> water, decrease in, 18–19

sweetness, comparison of, 50–51
Sweet'n Low, 51

V

vinegar, 45, 48–49, 52

W

water
> adhesive attraction, 26
> flowing pattern of, 30–31
> surface of, 20–21
> surface tension, 18–19, 31
> uphill movement of, 26–27

water drops, shape of, 24
water molecules, 14–15, 16, 18, 20
> motion of, 12–13

water surface, 23
> bulging of, 22–23
> dipping of, 20–21

wetting ability, 24–25
whey, 52